Here to Help

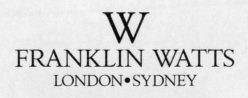

DENTIST

Rachel Blount

Photography by Bobby Humphrey

W
FRANKLIN WATTS
LONDON · SYDNEY

Franklin Watts
First published in Great Britain in 2017 by The Watts Publishing Group

Credits
Series Editor: Paul Humphrey
Series Designer: D. R. ink
Photographer: Bobby Humphrey
Produced for Franklin Watts by Discovery Books Ltd.

Dewey number: 617.6
ISBN: 978 1 4451 3997 5

Printed in China

Franklin Watts
An imprint of
Hachette Children's Group
Part of The Watts Publishing Group
Carmelite House
50 Victoria Embankment
London EC4Y 0DZ

An Hachette UK Company
www.hachette.co.uk
www.franklinwatts.co.uk

The publisher and packager would like to thank the following people for their help with this book: Paul Elliott and all staff at Northwick Manor Dental Practice, Worcester; Claire and Livie Thomas; Claire Smith and Henry Hemming.

Contents

I am a dentist   4

Special instruments   6

Getting ready   8

Henry's check-up   10

Check and polish   12

Looking after your teeth   14

My next patient   16

Having an X-ray   18

End of the day   20

Helping people   22

When you grow up... & Answers   23

Glossary & Index   24

Words in **bold** are in the glossary on page 24.

I am a dentist

My name is Paul
and I am a dentist.
It is my job to look
after people's teeth.
Here are some of the
people that help me
do my job.

Hello!

When did
you last go to
the dentist?

?

This is Sarah.
She is a **receptionist**.
Sarah welcomes people to the **dental surgery**.
She is very friendly. Sarah answers the telephone
and makes **appointments** for my patients.

Here I am with Sarah and the team of dentists and surgery staff that I work with.

Sharon - **Dental nurse**

Nicola - Dentist

Dina - Dental nurse

Roberta - Dental nurse

Jane - **Dental hygienist**

Paul - Dentist

Sarah - Receptionist

Special instruments

This is the surgery. It has a big chair for my patients, which moves up and down, backwards and forwards.

I have to use lots of special **instruments** to do my job. These are some of them.

Light

There is a large, bright light that I use to help me see inside a patient's mouth more clearly.

Probe

This is called a **probe**. It helps me check if teeth are healthy.

Polisher

This machine is a called a **polisher**. I use it to polish a patient's teeth. It makes a buzzing noise and **rotates** when I turn it on.

?

What do you think this tool is used for?

Getting ready

We make sure the surgery is clean and ready for each patient.

Dina gets the instruments ready for my first patient.

Why do you think dentists need dental nurses to help them?

After I have seen a patient, Dina uses the computer to make notes about the patient's teeth.

Dina helps me when I am doing my job. She passes me the correct instruments and helps me when I am working in the patient's mouth.

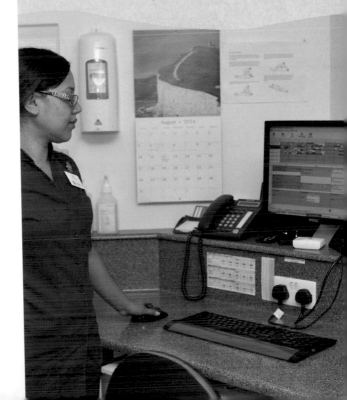

Henry's check-up

Henry, my next patient, is in the waiting room. Henry has come for a check-up. Dina brings him in.

I ask Henry and his mum about his teeth and whether he has been looking after them.

Have you been cleaning your teeth well?

Henry jumps into the big chair. Dina hands some **eye shields** to Henry to protect his eyes.

What three things can you remember about your first visit to the dentist?

I press a button so that Henry is lying flat.

Check and polish

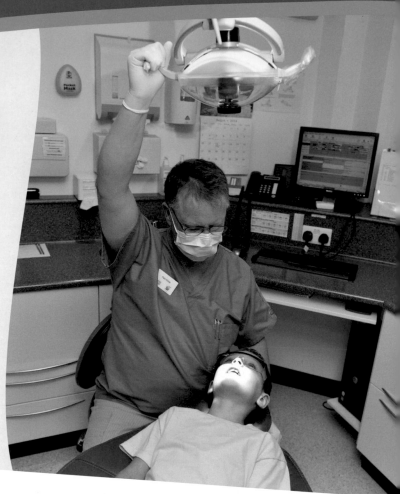

I shine the light into Henry's mouth and check his teeth, gums and mouth.

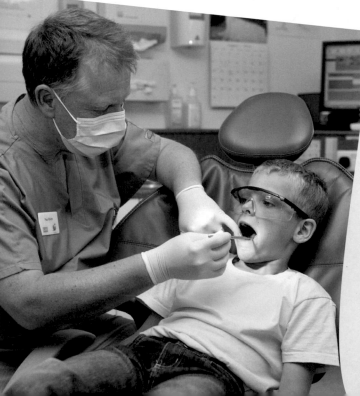

Next, I count Henry's teeth. He has 20 teeth. These are called his **milk teeth**. They are nice and clean. Henry has been looking after them.

Dina puts a bib on Henry to protect his clothes. I gently polish Henry's teeth to give them a nice shine.

We're nearly finished, Henry.

What does the mouthwash at the dentist's taste like?

Dina holds a **suction** machine, which sucks up any extra water in Henry's mouth. Henry rinses his mouth out with **mouthwash**.

schülke →

esemdent

Looking after your teeth

Jane, the dental hygienist, uses a plastic model of a mouth to show Henry how to brush in all the right places.

She uses a mirror to show Henry how to brush his own teeth properly.

It is very important not to eat too many sweets or sugary drinks. These things can be bad for your teeth. If you don't look after your teeth properly they can start to go rotten. This is called **tooth decay** and may mean you need a **filling**.

?

What is wrong with the toothbrush on the right?

We have finished Henry's check-up, so he chooses a sticker to wear.

My next patient

Livie is a bit nervous about visiting the dentist. Dina has a talk with her and explains what will happen. When Livie feels better, Dina brings her into the surgery.

?

What do your teeth feel like if you forget to brush them?

I'm a bit worried.

Do your teeth hurt at all?

I ask Livie about her teeth and if she has had any problems or toothache.

I look in Livie's mouth with the mirror. Her teeth are nice and clean but I need to check they are growing properly. To do this I need to take an **X-ray**.

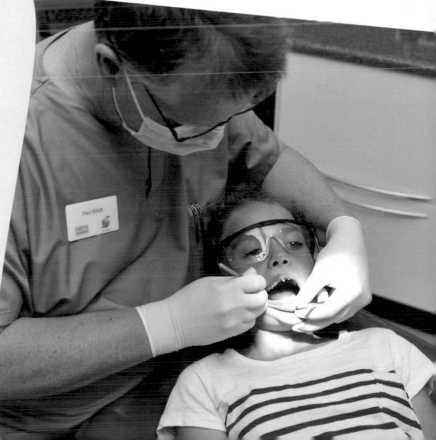

Having an X-ray

An X-ray is a special photograph. Dina gets the X-ray machine ready for Livie.

I place a small piece of plastic inside Livie's mouth, which she bites down on. The X-ray **film** is inside the plastic. I press a button to take the X-ray.

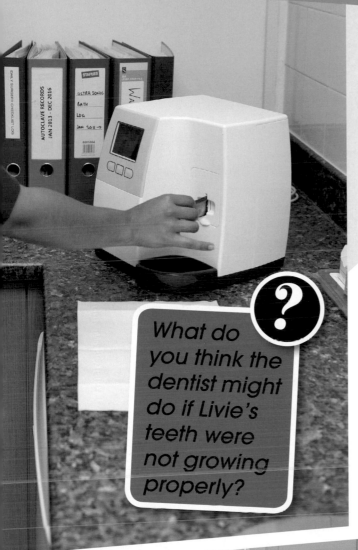

Dina takes the X-ray film to the **developing room**. The picture of Livie's teeth appears on my computer screen.

?

What do you think the dentist might do if Livie's teeth were not growing properly?

I can see that Livie's teeth are growing straight. I say goodbye to Livie and ask her to see me again in six months.

End of the day

It has been a busy day. I have seen twenty patients but my team and I still have work to do.

Dina cleans the surgery and gets the instruments and equipment clean for tomorrow. She puts the instruments into a machine called a **sterilizer**. This makes them very hot and kills any **germs**.

I check the computer and reply to any emails. I also look to see what appointments I have booked in for tomorrow.

Why do you think the dentist's instruments have to be cieaned after they have been used?

Helping people

I really enjoy my job as a dentist. I work with a great team of people who help me to do my job.

Most of all I enjoy helping people look after their teeth.

I really enjoy my job!

When you grow up...

If you would like to be a dentist, here are some simple tips and advice.

What kind of person are you?

- You are friendly and enjoy speaking to people
- You may be interested in the body and the way it works
- You are interested in science
- You are practical and like working with your hands
- Most of all, you enjoy helping people.

How do you become a dentist?

You will have to study science subjects at GCSE (Scottish Standard Grades) and at A Level (Scottish Highers). You will also have to study dentistry at university.

Answers

P7. The tool is a mirror. The mirror helps a dentist look at a patient's teeth, gums, tongue and the inside of their mouth.

P9. A dentist needs a dental nurse because there are too many things for one person to hold – an extra pair of hands is often needed.

P13. The mouthwash tastes like mint.

P15. The toothbrush on the right is worn out. The bristles are bent so they can't clean teeth properly.

P16. Your teeth can sometimes feel a bit furry if you forget to brush them.

P19. The dentist would speak with Livie. He might make an appointment for her to see a specialist dentist who will see whether she needs help to straighten her teeth.

P21. The dentist's instruments have to be cleaned every time they are used to kill germs that can make people ill.

Were your answers the same as the ones in this book? Don't worry if they were different, sometimes there is more than one right answer. Talk about your answer with other people. Can you explain why you think your answer is right?

Glossary

appointments meetings

dental hygienist someone who specialises in cleaning teeth and offers advice on how to look after teeth

dental nurse a specially trained nurse who helps a dentist do their job

dental surgery a place that people visit to see a dentist

developing room a room where photos or X-rays are developed

eye shields plastic glasses used to protect a patient's eyes

filling when a hole appears in a tooth it needs to be filled with a filling

film photographic film used to make X-rays

germs very small living things that can make people ill

instruments special tools used by dentists

milk teeth the first set of teeth a child grows

mouthwash a liquid used to rinse out the mouth (it also kills germs)

polisher an instrument that dentists use to polish teeth

probe a sharp, pointed, metal tool used by a dentist

receptionist someone who welcomes people to a surgery or office

rotates to move in a circular motion

sterilizer a machine that heats things up to kill germs

suction to remove by sucking

tooth decay when a tooth starts to go rotten

X-ray a special photograph

Index

appointments 5, 19, 21

brushing 14–15, 16

check-up 10–15

computer 9, 19, 21

dental hygienist 5, 14

dental nurse 5, 8, 9, 11, 13, 15, 16, 18, 19, 20

eye shields 11

fillings 15

germs 20

healthy eating 15

instruments 6–7, 8, 9, 12, 13, 17, 20, 21

looking after teeth 14–15

milk teeth 12

mirror 7, 17

mouthwash 13

polisher 7, 13

probe 7

receptionist 5

sterilizing 20

surgery 5, 6, 8, 16, 20

tooth decay 15

waiting room 10, 16

X-ray 17, 18–19